A Look at US History

# THE CIVIL RIGHTS MOVEMENT

BY JOHN O'MARA

Gareth Stevens
PUBLISHING

CRASH COURSE

Please visit our website, www.garethstevens.com. For a free color catalog of all our high-quality books, call toll free 1-800-542-2595 or fax 1-877-542-2596.

**Cataloging-in-Publication Data**

Names: O'Mara, John.
Title: The civil rights movement / John O'Mara.
Description: New York : Gareth Stevens Publishing, 2020. | Series: A look at U.S. history | Includes glossary and index.
Identifiers: ISBN 9781538248676 (pbk.) | ISBN 9781538248690 (library bound) | ISBN 9781538248683 (6 pack)
Subjects: LCSH: African Americans--Civil rights--History--Juvenile literature. | Civil rights movements--United States--History--20th century--Juvenile literature. | United States--Race relations--Juvenile literature.
Classification: LCC E185.61 O43 2020 | DDC 323.1196'073--dc23

First Edition

Published in 2020 by
**Gareth Stevens Publishing**
111 East 14th Street, Suite 349
New York, NY 10003

Copyright © 2020 Gareth Stevens Publishing

Editor: Therese Shea

Photo credits: Series art Christophe BOISSON/Shutterstock.com; (feather quill) Galushko Sergey/Shutterstock.com; (parchment) mollicart-design/Shutterstock.com; cover, p. 1 Express Newspapers/Hulton Archive/Getty Images; p. 5 Photo 12/Contributor/Getty Images; p. 7 Everett Historical/Shutterstock.com; p. 9 Universal History Archive/Getty Images; p. 11 FPG/Archive Photos /Getty Images; pp. 13, 15 Bettmann/Getty Images; p. 17 Don Cravens/The LIFE Images Collection/Getty Images; p. 19 John Melton/Oklahoma Historical Society/ Archive Photos/Getty Images; p. 21 Underwood Archives/Getty Images; p. 23 - / Contributor/AFP/Getty Images; p. 25 Cecil Stoughton, White House Press Office (WHPO)/ Wikimedia; p. 27 Hulton Archive/Getty Images; p. 29 Felix Lipov/Shutterstock.com.

All rights reserved. No part of this book may be reproduced in any form without permission in writing from the publisher, except by a reviewer.

Printed in the United States of America

Some of the images in this book illustrate individuals who are models. The depictions do not imply actual situations or events.

CPSIA compliance information: Batch #CW20GS: For further information contact Gareth Stevens, New York, New York at 1-800-542-2595.

# CONTENTS

| | |
|---|---|
| What Are Civil Rights? | 4 |
| The Rise of Jim Crow | 6 |
| *Brown v. Board of Education* | 12 |
| Rosa Parks and the Bus Boycott | 14 |
| Sit-Ins | 18 |
| Freedom Rides | 20 |
| The March on Washington | 22 |
| Civil Rights Laws | 24 |
| Malcolm X | 26 |
| The Movement Continues | 28 |
| Key Dates of the Civil Rights Movement | 30 |
| Glossary | 31 |
| For More Information | 32 |
| Index | 32 |

Words in the glossary appear in **bold** type the first time they are used in the text.

# WHAT ARE CIVIL RIGHTS?

Civil rights are rights that belong to a country's **citizens**. After the American Civil War (1861–1865), black Americans were made US citizens. However, their civil rights weren't respected. In the 1950s and 1960s, they began to fight for equal rights.

## MAKE THE GRADE

The Fourteenth **Amendment** of the US Constitution, the highest law in the nation, made all people born or **naturalized** in the United States citizens. This included former slaves.

5

# THE RISE OF JIM CROW

Beginning in the 1870s, some states passed laws that kept black Americans from voting. Black people had to take tests or pay money to vote. They often didn't have the schooling or money that white people had, so they couldn't vote.

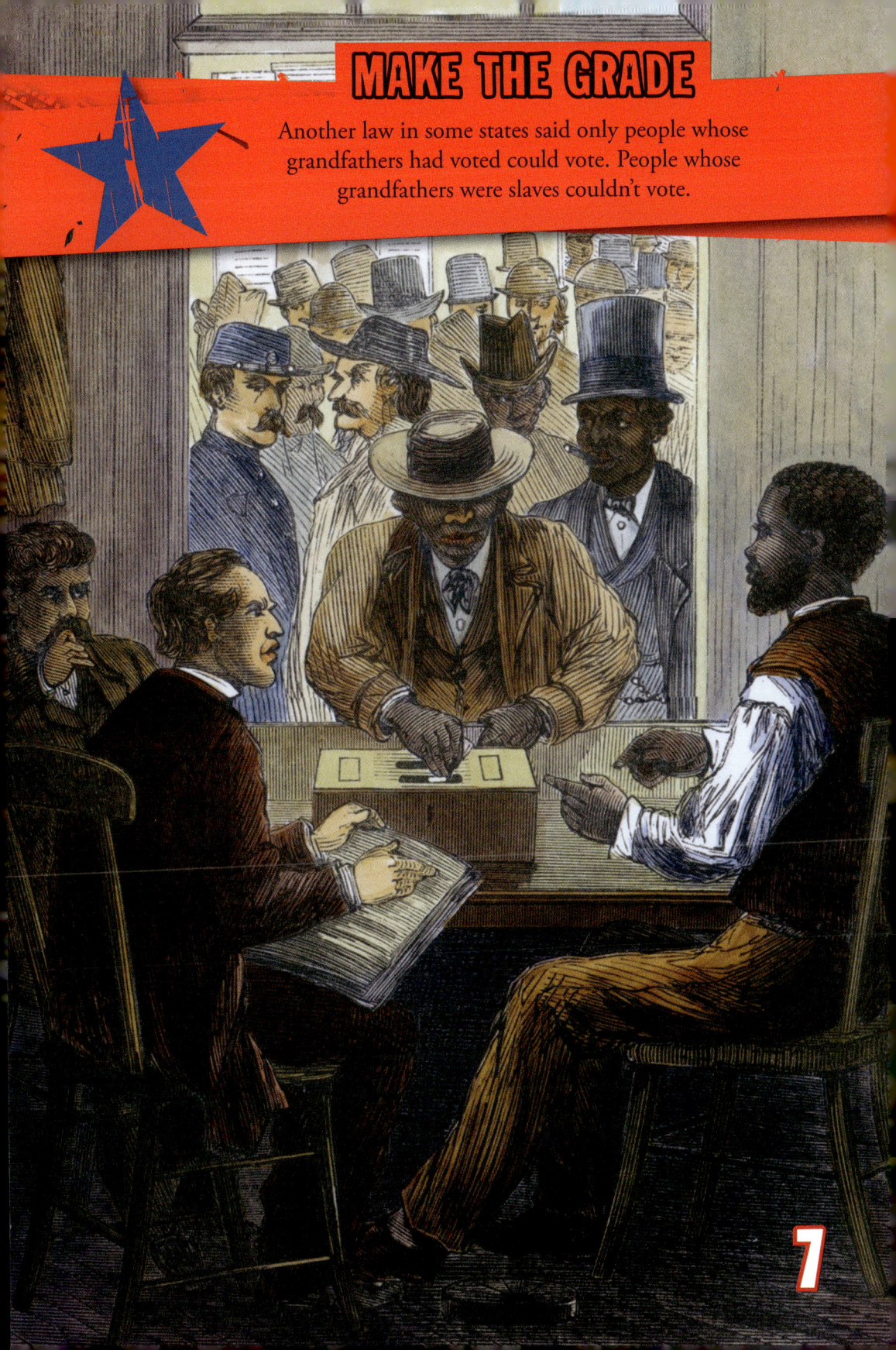

# MAKE THE GRADE

Another law in some states said only people whose grandfathers had voted could vote. People whose grandfathers were slaves couldn't vote.

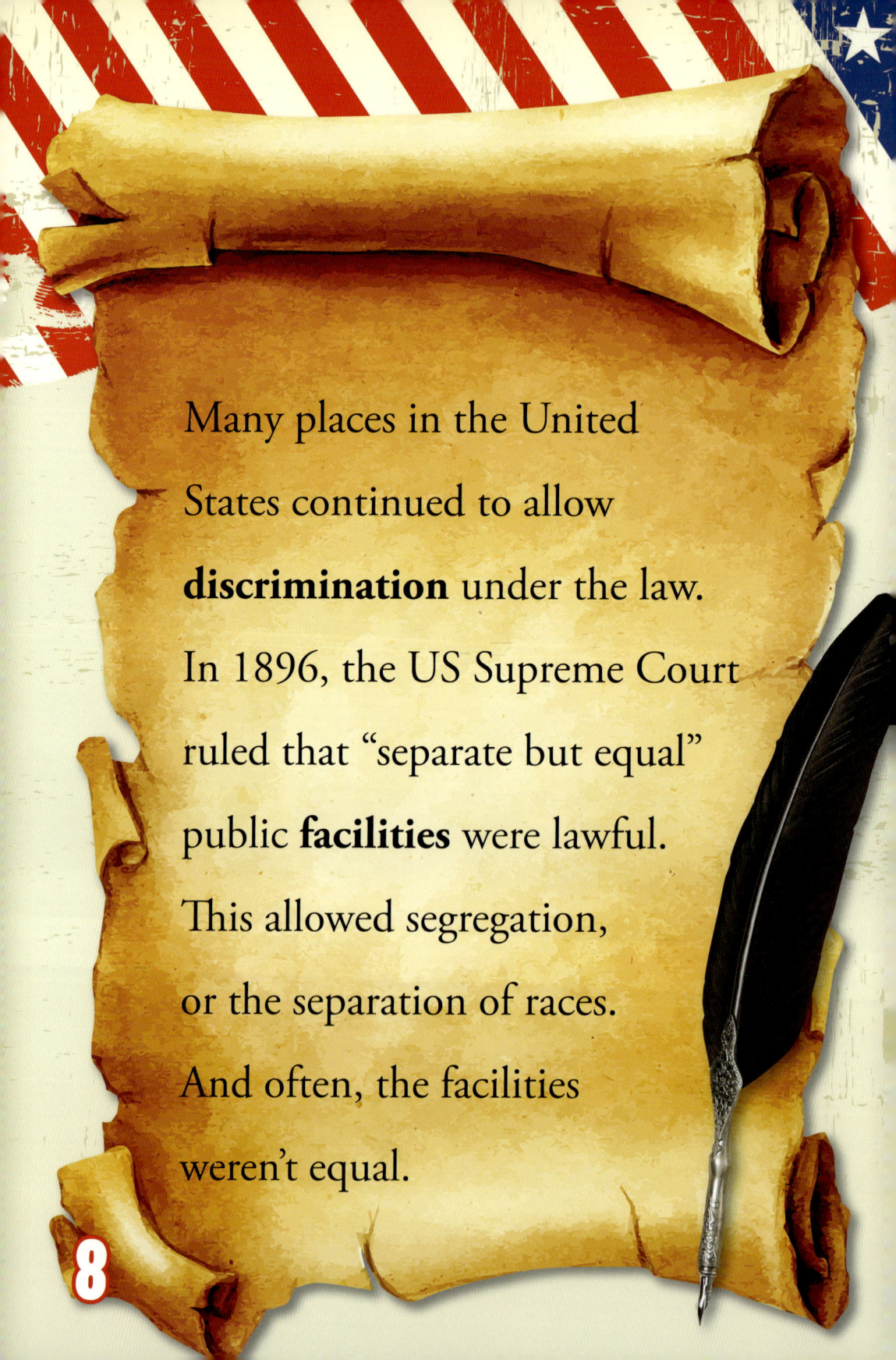

Many places in the United States continued to allow **discrimination** under the law. In 1896, the US Supreme Court ruled that "separate but equal" public **facilities** were lawful. This allowed segregation, or the separation of races. And often, the facilities weren't equal.

## MAKE THE GRADE

Civil rights include the right to vote, schooling, jobs, housing, government services, and more.

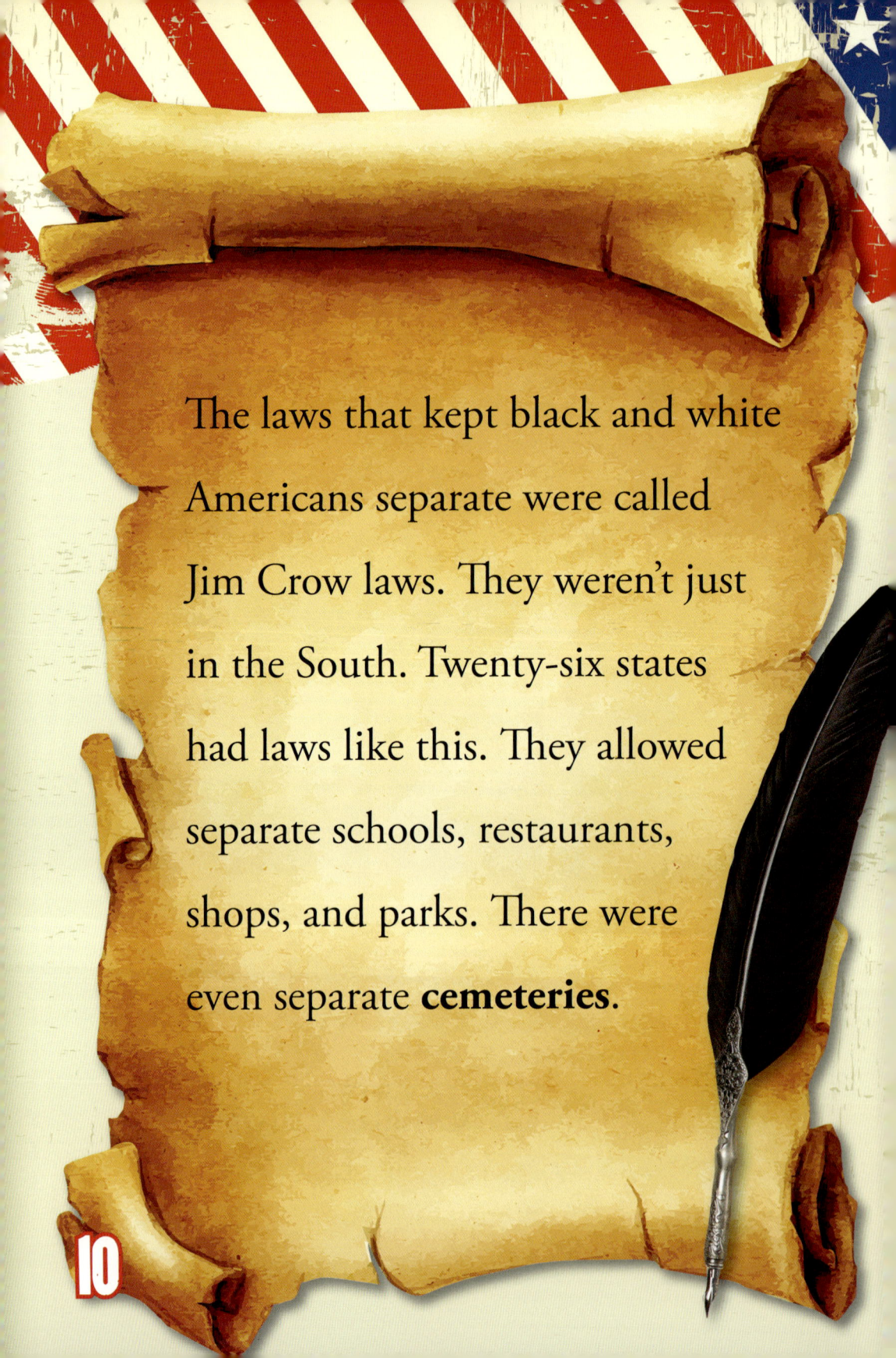

The laws that kept black and white Americans separate were called Jim Crow laws. They weren't just in the South. Twenty-six states had laws like this. They allowed separate schools, restaurants, shops, and parks. There were even separate **cemeteries**.

## MAKE THE GRADE

In places with Jim Crow laws, there were often signs on doorways and other objects. Some said "whites only." Others used the word "colored," which is **offensive** today.

# BROWN V. BOARD OF EDUCATION

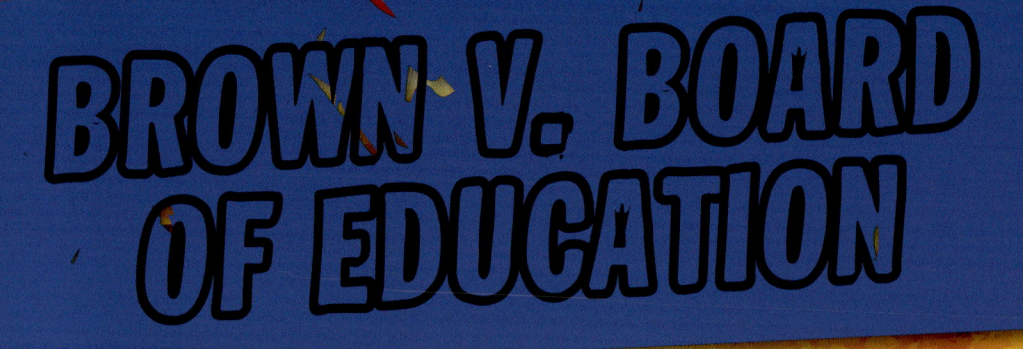

The National Association for the Advancement of Colored People (NAACP) fought for equality through court cases. A case called *Brown v. Board of Education of Topeka* reached the highest US court, the Supreme Court. In 1954, it ruled "separate but equal" schools were **unconstitutional**.

## MAKE THE GRADE

NAACP **lawyer** Thurgood Marshall, center, proved that white schools and black schools weren't equal. He later became a Supreme Court justice, or judge.

13

# Rosa Parks and the Bus Boycott

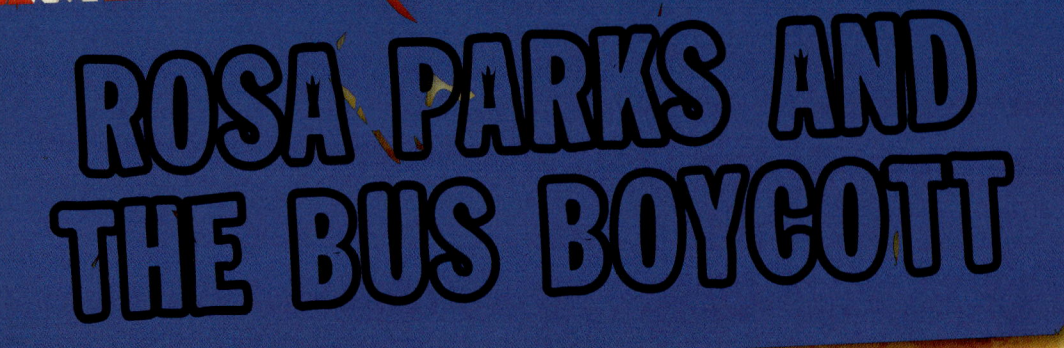

Still, segregation remained a way of life in many parts of the United States. In 1955, a black woman in Montgomery, Alabama, named Rosa Parks refused to give her bus seat to a white man. She was arrested. People decided to take action.

# Rosa Parks

## MAKE THE GRADE

In Montgomery, black people were supposed to sit in the back of the bus. If the front was full, they were supposed to give their seats to white people.

15

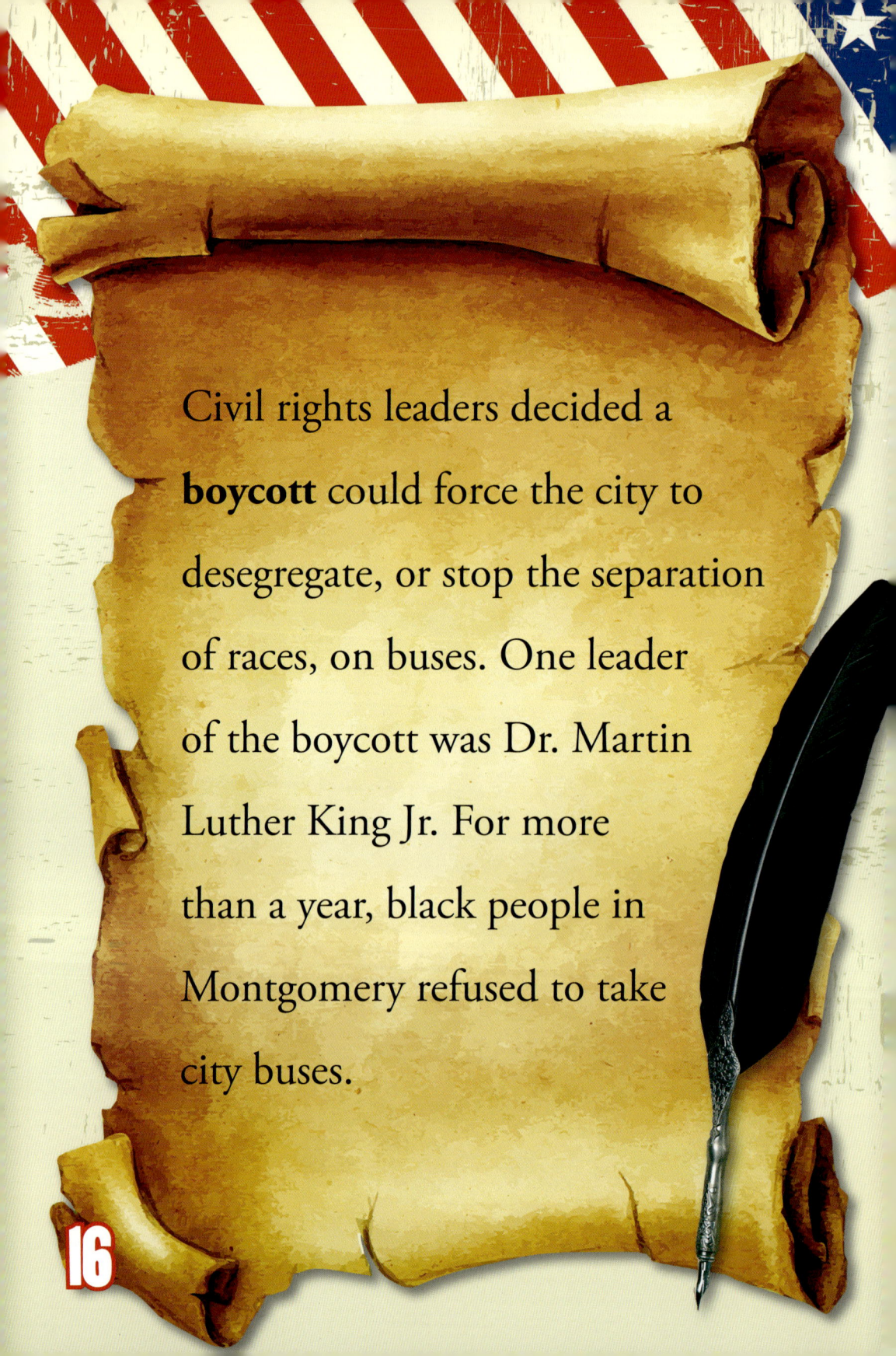

Civil rights leaders decided a **boycott** could force the city to desegregate, or stop the separation of races, on buses. One leader of the boycott was Dr. Martin Luther King Jr. For more than a year, black people in Montgomery refused to take city buses.

# Martin Luther King Jr.

## MAKE THE GRADE

In 1956, the Supreme Court finally ruled that bus segregation was unconstitutional.

# SIT-INS

Leaders of the civil rights movement fought against other areas of segregation. One of the ways they did this was called a sit-in. During this peaceful **protest**, people sat in segregated places such as restaurants and businesses until they were served.

## MAKE THE GRADE

Fifteen-year-old Barbara Posey, pictured above, was a leader of sit-ins at segregated lunch counters in Oklahoma, beginning in 1958.

# FREEDOM RIDES

In 1960, the Supreme Court ruled segregation wasn't lawful in bus stations and restrooms. To fight segregation that was still taking place, supporters of the civil rights movement began Freedom Rides. They rode buses through the South, using facilities they weren't supposed to.

## MAKE THE GRADE

Some of the Freedom Riders were arrested. Some were beaten. One bus they rode through Alabama was set on fire.

# THE MARCH ON WASHINGTON

On August 28, 1963, more than 200,000 people gathered in Washington, DC, to show support for the civil rights movement. Martin Luther King Jr. gave his powerful "I Have a Dream" speech. Many people were moved by his words and asked for new equality laws.

## MAKE THE GRADE

King said, "I have a dream that my four little children will one day live in a nation where they will not be judged by the color of their skin but by the content of their character."

# CIVIL RIGHTS LAWS

In 1964, the US Congress passed the Civil Rights Act to fight discrimination based on race, color, **religion**, or the country someone came from. It also banned segregation in public places. The Voting Rights Act of 1965 banned practices that stopped black Americans from voting.

# MAKE THE GRADE

President Lyndon B. Johnson signed both the Civil Rights Act of 1964 and the Voting Rights Act of 1965 into law.

# MALCOLM X

Not everyone believed in the peaceful methods of Martin Luther King Jr. and the civil rights movement. Malcolm X, for example, thought more forceful methods might be needed. He spoke powerfully of black pride and had many followers.

## MAKE THE GRADE

Toward the end of his life, Malcolm X believed all races could live peacefully together. On February 21, 1965, he was assassinated, or killed.

# The Movement Continues

On April 4, 1968, Martin Luther King Jr. was assassinated in Memphis, Tennessee. He had been working to help the poor of all races. The civil rights movement didn't end with King's death, but it was never as **united** again.

**Martin Luther King Jr. Memorial
Washington, DC**

## MAKE THE GRADE

After King's death, some black Americans joined **militant** groups such as the Black Panther Party. Others began to seek change through government positions.

# KEY DATES OF THE CIVIL RIGHTS MOVEMENT

**1954**
The Supreme Court rules "separate but equal" is unconstitutional in *Brown v. Board of Education of Topeka*.

**1955**
Rosa Parks is arrested in Montgomery, Alabama, for not giving up her bus seat. A bus boycott begins.

**1958**
Sit-in protests begin in Oklahoma City, Oklahoma.

**1961**
The first Freedom Rides take place.

**1963**
The March on Washington takes place. Martin Luther King Jr. gives his "I Have a Dream" speech.

**1964**
The Civil Rights Act is passed.

**1965**
Malcolm X is killed. The Voting Rights Act is passed.

**1968**
Martin Luther King Jr. is assassinated.

# GLOSSARY

**amendment:** a change or addition to a constitution

**boycott:** the act of refusing to have dealings with a person or business to force change

**cemetery:** a place where the dead are buried

**citizen:** someone who lives in a country legally and has certain rights

**discrimination:** unfairly treating people unequally because of their race or beliefs

**facility:** something built for a purpose

**lawyer:** someone who helps people with questions and problems with the law

**militant:** describing a group who will use force to support a cause or beliefs

**naturalized:** describing someone born in a different country who becomes a citizen

**offensive:** causing someone to feel hurt, angry, or upset

**protest:** an event at which a group objects to an idea, act, or way of doing something

**religion:** a belief in and way of honoring a god or gods

**unconstitutional:** describing something that goes against the US Constitution

**united:** working together to achieve a goal

# For More Information

## Books

Braun, Eric. *The Civil Rights Movement*. Minneapolis, MN: Lerner Publications, 2019.

Shabazz, Ilyasah. *Malcolm Little: The Boy Who Grew Up to Become Malcolm X*. New York, NY: Atheneum Books for Young Readers, 2014.

## Websites

**Civil Rights for Kids**
www.ducksters.com/history/civil_rights/
Read more about civil rights and the people who have fought for them.

**Martin Luther King Jr.**
kids.nationalgeographic.com/explore/history/martin-luther-king-jr/
Discover more about Dr. King's life.

**Publisher's note to educators and parents:** Our editors have carefully reviewed these websites to ensure that they are suitable for students. Many websites change frequently, however, and we cannot guarantee that a site's future contents will continue to meet our high standards of quality and educational value. Be advised that students should be closely supervised whenever they access the internet.

## INDEX

Civil War 4
*Brown v. Board of Education of Topeka* 12, 30
bus boycott 14, 30
Civil Rights Act 24, 25, 30
Freedom Rides 20, 30
"I Have a Dream" speech 22, 23, 30
Jim Crow laws 6, 10, 11
King, Martin Luther, Jr. 16, 22, 26, 28, 30
Malcolm X 26, 27, 30
Parks, Rosa 14, 30
sit-ins 18
Voting Rights Act 24, 25, 30